Wise Words from David Attenborough

Illustrations by Nat Carroll

Harper *by* Design

Introduction

In 1954, a young television producer at the BBC named David Attenborough found himself in front of the camera after originally being advised that his teeth were possibly too big for on-screen. The show's original presenter had recently returned from a work trip to Africa with a mysterious illness and was too unwell to work.

Since that day, in a much-celebrated career spanning eight decades, Sir David Attenborough has charmed, delighted and informed us about the natural world all around us and the associated effects of human society, from the remote forests of Rwanda inhabited by endangered mountain gorillas to the plight of the Great Barrier Reef and the irreversible impact of climate change.

Knighted twice and awarded over thirty honorary university degrees, David is one of the most well-travelled people on Earth. He has been called the greatest broadcaster of our time, the great communicator and having influenced an entire generation of wildlife filmmakers. Fellow presenter, naturalist and author Chris Packham puts it best: 'David tells stories so that they become irresistible to us. We want to know what happens. We care because we trust him ... he is an expert and he is so very passionate.'

That spirit is reflected in this collection of quotes from the world's most popular conservationist and writer. Each has helped shift the conversation forward in some way, shape or form. There will never be another David Attenborough, with his irreplaceable blend of enthusiasm and knowledge, but it is impossible not to hear his voice when reading through these pages.

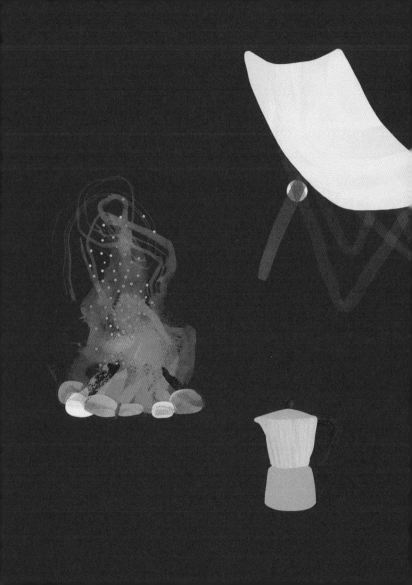

The natural world then seemed

like an unexplored world ...

everywhere you turned

you saw something new.

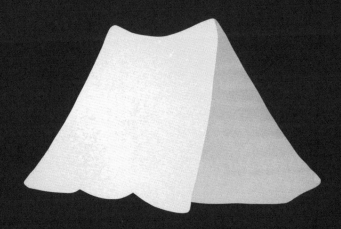

What we do in the next few years

will profoundly affect

the next few thousand years.

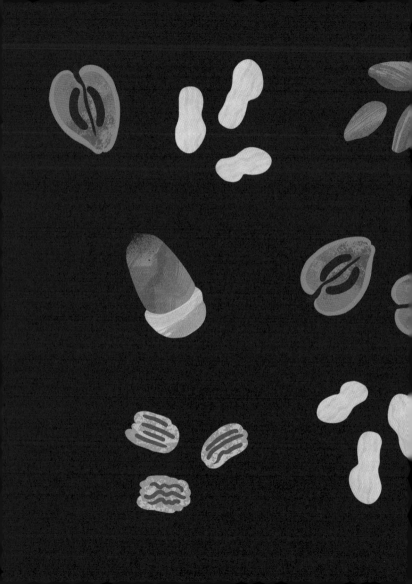

Every breath of air we take,

every mouthful of food we take,

comes from the natural world.

Care for the natural world ...

treat it with a degree of respect

and reverence.

The future of the natural world

is in our hands.

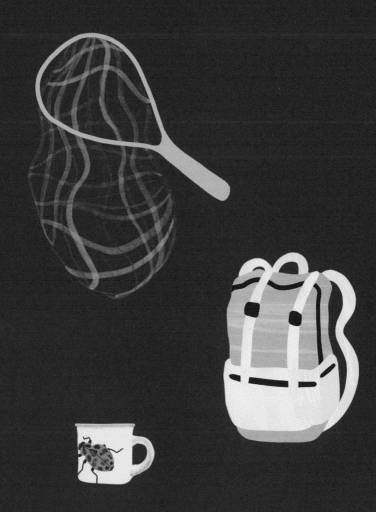

[I'm] not a feminist. I'm a humanist. I'm neither one side nor the other. It's about the human being.

We should feel guilty

for the way we've
treated the planet.

Bring on electric cars.

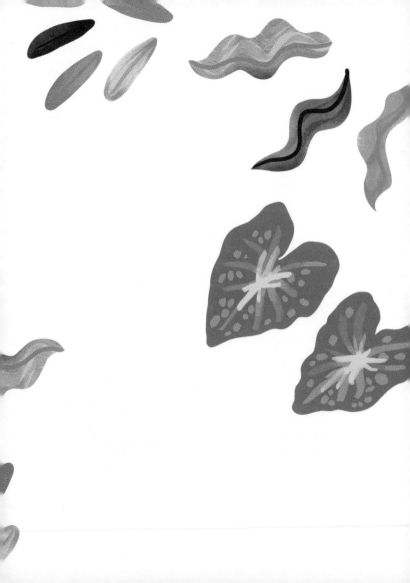

If we were all to reduce

our demands for energy,

it would make an enormous

amount of difference.

The job ... is really pretty easy.

Because the animals

are so fantastic.

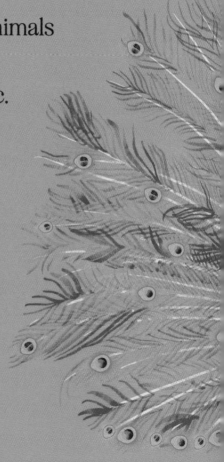

We depend upon the natural world for every mouthful of food that we eat and indeed every lungful of air that we breathe.

The story of how life

developed on this planet

... is the greatest story ever told.

People ... need the natural world

for their very sanity.

If there were no trees around

we would suffocate.

We all know in our heart of hearts

how important the natural world is.

In the most hostile environments

that you can imagine, there is some

little creature beavering away there,

just earning a living.

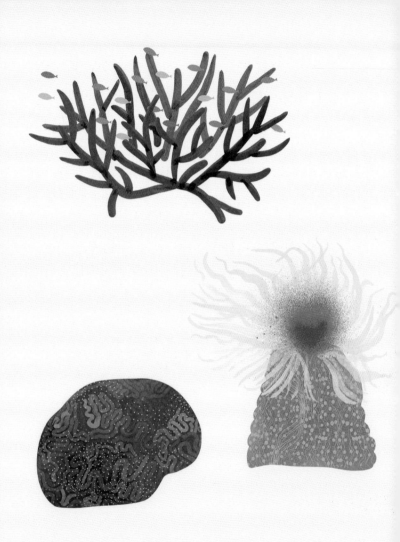

Why would I want
to go and live on the
Moon when I've got
this world of badgers
and thrushes and
jellyfish and corals?

Either we limit our population growth

or the natural world

will do it for us.

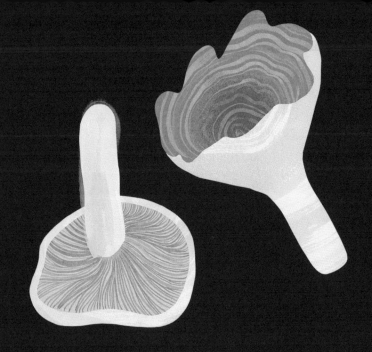

We must change our diet.

The planet can't support billions

of meat-eaters.

Fig. 1.

Fig. 2

Nature once determined how we survive.

Now we determine

how nature survives.

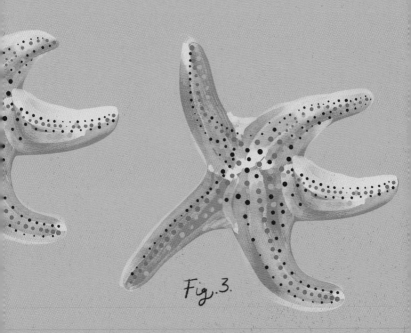

Fig. 3.

Those who've done the least

to cause this problem,

are being the hardest hit.

Nature is a key ally.

Whenever we restore the wild,

it will recapture carbon

and help us bring back

balance to our planet.

I just wish the world was twice as big and half of it was still unexplored.

WISE WORDS FROM DAVID ATTENBOROUGH

60

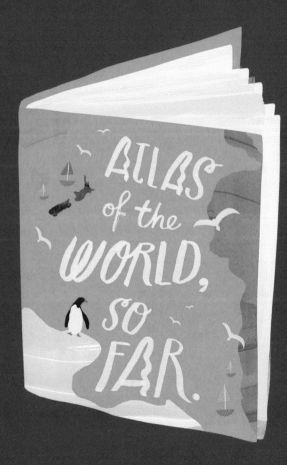

No nation has completed

its development

because no advanced nation

is yet sustainable.

One of the most magical moments

of a naturalist's life is the first time

you dive on a coral reef.

I've always got to remember

that I'll forget something.

Surely, working together,

we are powerful enough

to save [our planet].

Movements and ideas can spread

at astonishing speed.

Our motivation should not be fear, but hope.

WISE WORDS FROM DAVID ATTENBOROUGH

77

I still collect fossils ...

that wonderful pleasure

in knocking a rock open

to see one inside.

I still recall like yesterday the

feeling of being a young man ...

I feel exactly the same.

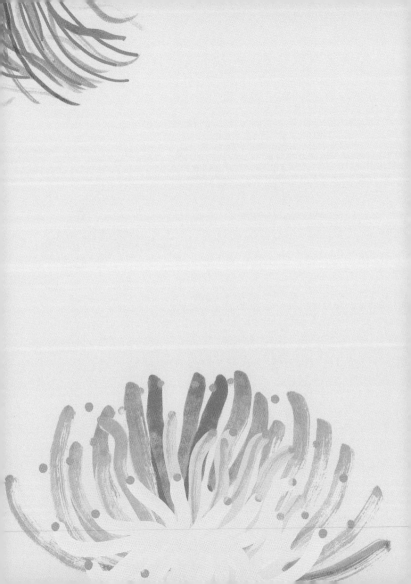

The Earth and its oceans

are finite.

We need more than just intelligence,

we need wisdom.

After all, this planet is all we have.

There is nowhere else to go.

About the illustrator

Nat Carroll is an Australian artist. She creates illustrations and lettering for publishing, murals, textiles, brands, as well as her own art brand. Her practice is a sparkly, colourful ode to the wonder and joy she stumbles upon in her universe. A dream-like, emotive language of place, nature, words and people are playfully explored from her studio next to the ocean, amongst the trees on the south-east coast of Australia, on Djiringanj Country.

Nat's work has featured in publications including Semi-Permanent and Curvy, exhibited in galleries including aMBUSH Gallery and Tinning St Gallery, and has been shortlisted in Cannes Lions. Some of the lovely folks she's worked with include the ABC, Adelaide Women & Children's Hospital, DDB, Frankie Mag, HarperCollins, Harvard Business Review, Reach Out, triple j and Westpac.

Swimming, reading, plant-hoarding, travelling and wandering with her doggo in the forest keep her feeling human.

Harper *by* Design

An imprint of HarperCollins*Publishers*

HarperCollins*Publishers*
Australia • Brazil • Canada • France • Germany • Holland • India
Italy • Japan • Mexico • New Zealand • Poland • Spain • Sweden
Switzerland • United Kingdom • United States of America

HarperCollins acknowledges the Traditional Custodians of the lands upon
which we live and work, and pays respect to Elders past and present.

First published on Gadigal Country in Australia in 2023
by HarperCollinsPublishers Australia Pty Limited
ABN 36 009 913 517
harpercollins.com.au

This is an unauthorised book of quotes

A catalogue record for this book is available from the National Library of Australia

ISBN 978 1 4607 6336 0

Publisher: Mark Campbell
Publishing Director: Brigitta Doyle
Project Editor: Chris Kunz
Designer: Mietta Yans, HarperCollins Design Studio
Illustrator: Nat Carroll
Colour reproduction by Splitting Image Colour Studio, Wantirna VIC

8 7 6 5 4 3   24 25 26 27